FUN WITH

SIMPLE SCIENCE

Sound and Music

BARBARA TAYLOR

WARWICK PRESS

SOUND AND MUSIC

In this book, you can discover how we hear sounds and find out how to make music by plucking strings, blowing down pipes, and hitting percussion instruments, such as drums.

The book is divided into seven different topics. Look out for the big headings with a circle at each end—like the one at the top of this page. These headings tell you where a new topic starts.

Pages 4–9

Sounds all Around

Everyday sounds; what is sound? How sound travels through solids, water, or air.

Pages 10–15

Loud and Quiet Sounds

Decibel scale; testing your hearing; megaphones and stethoscopes.

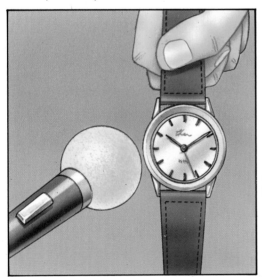

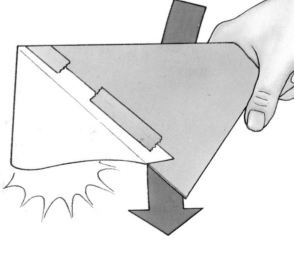

Pages 16–23

Drums, Scrapers, Shakers

Percussion instruments: drums; xylophones; chimes; maracas.

SOUNDS ALL AROUND

Make a tape recording of the everyday sounds around you. You could include sounds such as a door banging, a clock ticking, a bell ringing, or the sounds made by people, pets, or traffic. Try to record sounds indoors and out of doors.

Play the tape back to a friend. Can they recognize all the different sounds? Can you think of words to describe the sounds? Make up a poem or a story which includes all the sounds on the tape.

▶ In a noisy place, such as a fairground, it is hard to pick out individual sounds.

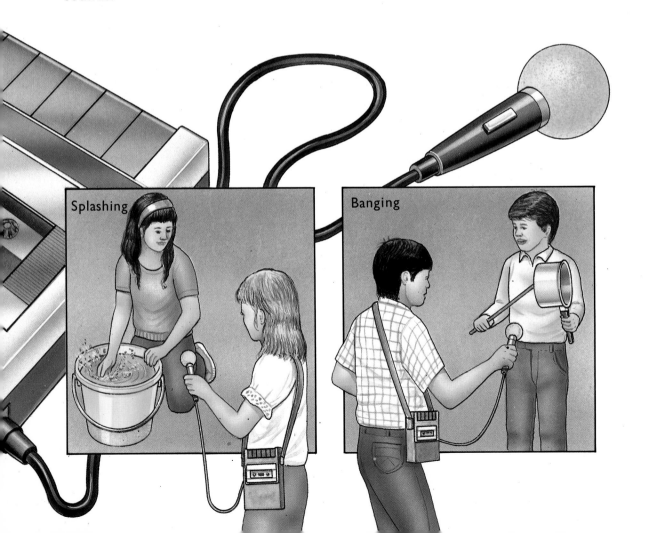

Splashing

Banging

Rustling

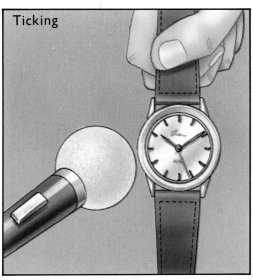

Ticking

Making Sounds

Make a collection of different materials, such as tissue paper, sandpaper, foil, cardboard, wood, plastic, sponge, and glass. Put up a screen and ask your friends to sit on one side of the screen. On the other side of the screen, make sounds with the materials in your collection. How many different ways of making sounds can you discover? Can your friends guess which materials you are using each time?

Sound on the Move

Find a long length of iron railings and ask a friend to stand at one end while you stand at the other end. When your friend taps the railings with a stick, can you hear the sound? Now put your ear close to the railings and repeat the experiment. What happens to the sound?

Sounds Underwater

Blow up a balloon and hold it next to your ear. Hold a watch on the other side of the balloon. Can you hear the watch ticking? Now fill the balloon with water and repeat the experiment. Does the water make the sound louder or quieter?

Sound travels about four times faster through water than it does through air. The sound of the watch should be louder through the water-filled balloon.

What Happens
Sounds travel faster through solid materials, such as the iron railings, than they do through air. So when you put your ear to the railings, the sound seems much louder. Try the same experiment with a brick wall instead of iron railings. You could make up a code of long and short taps and send messages.

Feeling Sounds

Sounds are invisible. You can't see them. But you can feel the way sounds make the air shake to and fro. These shaking movements are called vibrations. Rest two fingers lightly against your throat and say something. Can you feel the sound vibrations? When something vibrates fast, it makes high sounds. When something vibrates more slowly, the sounds are lower.

To feel the sounds made by a radio or cassette recorder, blow up a balloon and hold it in front of the loudspeakers. Compare the vibrations made by different kinds of music and loud and quiet music. Do the vibrations feel different?

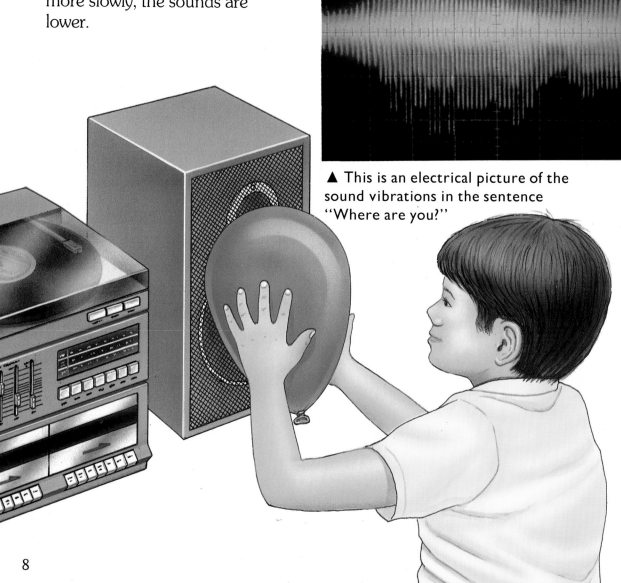

▲ This is an electrical picture of the sound vibrations in the sentence "Where are you?"

Seeing Sounds

To see a picture of your voice, try this experiment.

You will need:

a balloon, scissors, a short cardboard tube, a rubber band, a small piece of foil, a flashlight, glue, a plain wall or piece of cardboard.

1. Cut off the neck of the balloon and stretch the rest of the balloon tightly over one end of the tube. Use the rubber band to hold the balloon in place.
2. Glue the small piece of foil onto the balloon skin.
3. Shine the torch onto the foil at an angle so you can see a bright spot of light reflected onto the wall or cardboard.
4. Speak into the open end of the tube. Try high and low sounds as well as loud and quiet sounds. What happens to the light spot?

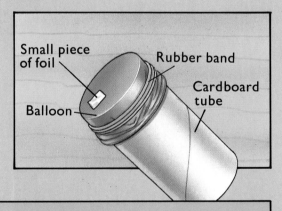

Small piece of foil

Rubber band

Cardboard tube

Balloon

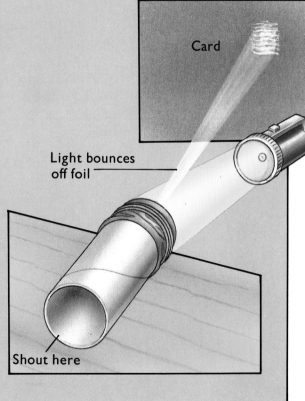

Card

Light bounces off foil

Shout here

What happens

The vibrations from your voice make the air in the tube vibrate. The air vibrations make the balloon skin and the reflected light vibrate too. You see the vibrations as streaks and wavy lines on the light spot.

LOUD AND QUIET SOUNDS

What is the loudest sound you have ever heard? Was it made by an airplane, a siren, or thunder during a storm? How many quiet sounds can you think of? Here are some ideas to get you started: footsteps on the carpet, a ticking watch, a mouse squeaking.

Draw a chart of objects that make loud sounds and objects that make quiet sounds. Do the objects in each group have anything in common?

The loudness of a sound is measured in units called decibels. Here is the decibel scale *(right)*. Did you know that a humpback whale can make a noise louder than a jet plane on take-off? (190 decibels)

Decibel Scale	
0	humans can just hear sounds
10	rustling leaves
20	whisper
60	normal conversation
80	heavy traffic
100	jackhammer
110	discotheque
120	jet airplane

▶ We call sounds we don't want or don't like noise. Very loud noise can damage our ears. People who work in noisy places should wear ear muffs to protect their ears.

Make your own ear muffs from foil cake cases or empty boxes. Hold them over your ears or use a hair band, rubber bands, or shoe laces to fix them in position. To cut out even more noise, try padding out the inside of the ear muffs with cotton balls, or tissue paper.

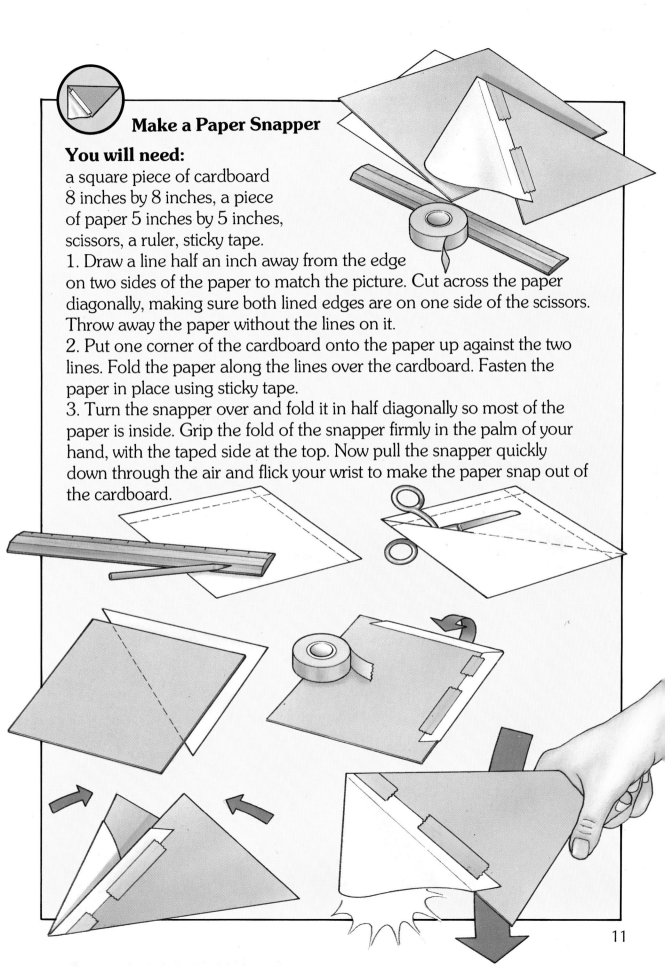

Make a Paper Snapper

You will need:

a square piece of cardboard
8 inches by 8 inches, a piece
of paper 5 inches by 5 inches,
scissors, a ruler, sticky tape.

1. Draw a line half an inch away from the edge
on two sides of the paper to match the picture. Cut across the paper
diagonally, making sure both lined edges are on one side of the scissors.
Throw away the paper without the lines on it.

2. Put one corner of the cardboard onto the paper up against the two
lines. Fold the paper along the lines over the cardboard. Fasten the
paper in place using sticky tape.

3. Turn the snapper over and fold it in half diagonally so most of the
paper is inside. Grip the fold of the snapper firmly in the palm of your
hand, with the taped side at the top. Now pull the snapper quickly
down through the air and flick your wrist to make the paper snap out of
the cardboard.

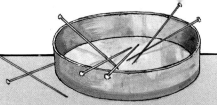

How Well Can You Hear?

Can you hear a pin drop? Ask a friend to stand with their back to a table and drop a pin onto the table. If they can hear the sound, they should put up one hand. Ask your friend to move away from the table two paces at a time until they can no longer hear the pin drop. Use a ruler to make sure you drop the pin from the same height each time. How far away can they still hear the pin?

Now try dropping a coin on to a different surface, such as carpet, grass, concrete, wood, or metal. On which material does the coin make the loudest sound? Make a list of all the materials. Arrange the list in order from the loudest to the quietest materials.

Animal Hearing

Most people can hear sounds from about 20 to 17,000 vibrations per second. But some animals can hear higher or lower sounds than we can. Dogs can hear the sounds made by special whistles, and cats can hear the squeaks of mice, which are too high for us to hear.

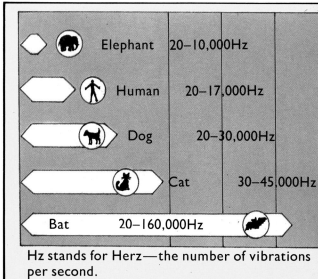

Elephant	20–10,000Hz		
Human		20–17,000Hz	
Dog		20–30,000Hz	
Cat			30–45,000Hz
Bat	20–160,000Hz		

Hz stands for Herz—the number of vibrations per second.

Two Ears are Better than One

To work out the direction of a sound, we compare the loudness of the sound reaching each ear. Some animals, such as rabbits, can swivel their ears to listen to sounds. This helps them to escape danger. Can you move your ears?

Can you guess the direction of a sound made by a friend when you are wearing a blindfold? The blindfold will help you to concentrate on the sounds. Try the same test with one ear covered. Are two ears better than one? Can you hear better with one ear than the other?

Making Sounds Louder

Cup your hands and hold them behind your ears. Can you hear better with your big ears? Now try holding your hands in front of your ears with the palms facing backward. Can you hear the sounds behind you more easily? How many animals can you think of with big ears?

Make a Stethoscope

Push a plastic funnel onto each end of a long piece of plastic or rubber tubing. Then ask a friend to hold one funnel over their chest while you hold the other funnel to your ear. Can you hear your friend's heart beating?
A doctor uses a stethoscope like this to listen to sounds inside the body. This helps the doctor to find out about a person's health.

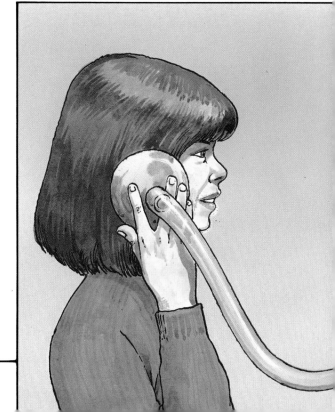

Making a Trumpet . . . and a Megaphone

Make an ear trumpet by rolling a large sheet of paper into a cone shape. Hold the thin end of the trumpet to your ear. The cone collects sounds and makes them seem louder. With an ear trumpet in each ear, can you hear twice as well? Do large trumpets work better than small ones? How many musical instruments can you think of which include a trumpet?

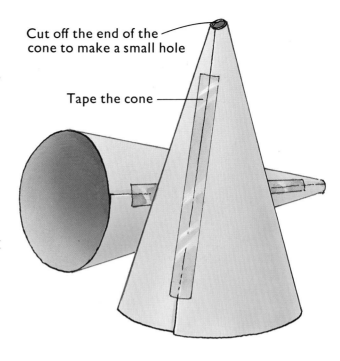

Cut off the end of the cone to make a small hole

Tape the cone

To make a megaphone, shout into the narrow end. The cone makes your voice seem louder.

Ask a friend to shout into a megaphone while you listen with an ear trumpet. How far away can you hear the sound of your friend's voice?

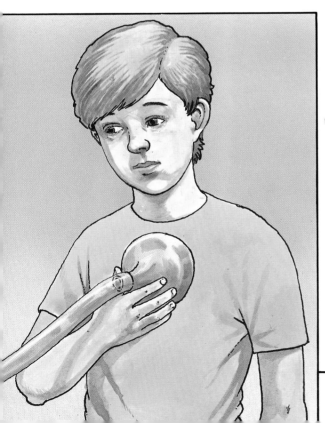

Instead of funnels, ask an adult to cut off the tops of two plastic bottles, as shown here.

Many musical instruments produce sounds when they are hit. These are called percussion instruments. The name comes from the word "percuss," which means to strike. They include drums, cymbals, triangles, tambourines, and xylophones.

 Making Drums

You can use a box or any hollow container as a drum. To make a drum that gives out different notes, you need a drum skin. Cut a piece out of a plastic bag and stretch it over a plastic bowl. Use tape or string to hold the bag in place. If you stretch the skin tighter, the plastic skin will vibrate faster and make a higher note.

Try making a drumskin from different materials, such as cloth, a balloon, or paper soaked in wallpaper paste to make it go hard. Which materials make the best sounds? Which materials last longest?

Try putting a few grains of rice on top of the drum. When you tap the drum, the sound makes the drum shake and the rice jumps up in the air. When the drum skin is stretched tighter, does the rice jump higher in the air?

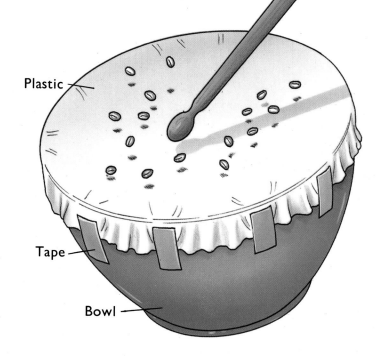

Plastic

Tape

Bowl

▲ Kettle drums or timpani have screws or a pedal to tighten the skin and change the note.

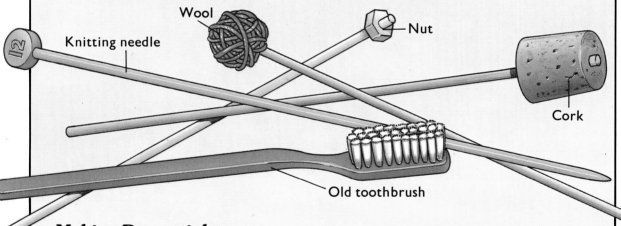

Wool

Nut

Knitting needle

Cork

Old toothbrush

Making Drumsticks

You can make different sounds with the same drum by using different ends on the drumsticks. Here are some ideas to try:
wooden beads, cork, a cloth, wool, sponge, a nut, bristles from a toothbrush or a hairbrush.

Fix the ends to the drumsticks with tape or rubber bands. Cloth or sponge ends make a quiet sound. Beads make a louder sound. What sort of sound do the bristles make? Which sound do you like best?

This West African drum is called a waisted drum because it has a narrow "waist" in the middle. By pressing on the lacing that joins the two skins, the drummer can change the note.

Make a Prayer Drum

1. Soak the brown paper in the paste and leave it to dry.
2. In the sides of the box or tub, cut two holes opposite each other and push the stick or dowel through the holes. Hold the wood in place with tape or clay.
3. Make two small holes in the other sides of the box. Thread one piece of string through each hole and tie a knot to keep the string in place.
4. Cut off the bottom of the box or tub.
5. To make the drumskins, tape a piece of the brown paper over each end of the box.
6. Pull each string across the drumskins in turn and mark where it reaches the middle. Tie a bead onto the string at this point.
7. Paint the sides of the drum with a pattern that you like, and leave it to dry.
8. To play the drum, twist the stick between your fingers so the beads hit the drumskin.

Prayer drums are used in religious ceremonies in countries such as Indonesia.

You will need:

a round, wooden box or a round plastic margarine tub, strong brown paper 12 inches by 12 inches, wallpaper paste, sticky tape, string, two wooden beads, dowel or a stick, a pencil, paints and paintbrushes, scissors, modeling clay.

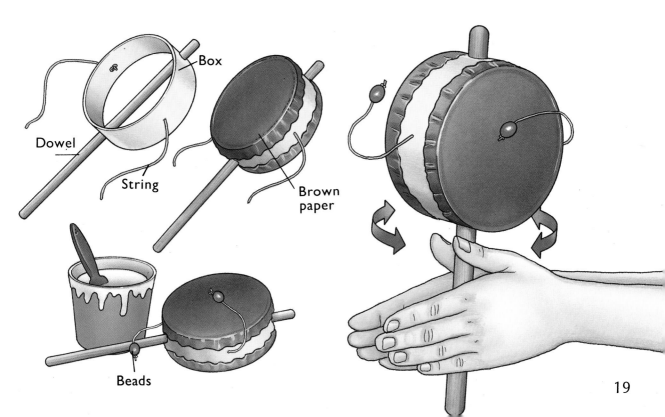

Dowel

Box

String

Brown paper

Beads

Making Scrapers

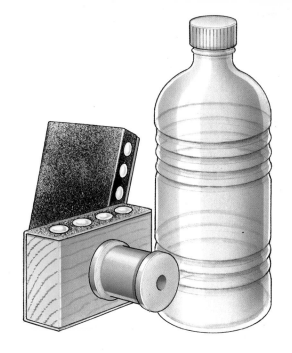

A plastic bottle with ridges along the sides makes a good scraper. Try using different objects, such as metal spoons, pencils, or stones to scrape along the ridges.

You can make another kind of scraper from two wooden blocks with sandpaper pinned on top. To make a handle for each scraper, glue a thread spool to the back of the block. Paint the backs of the scrapers with bright patterns. To make scraping sounds, hold one block in each hand and rub the sandpaper sides together.

Make different sized pairs of scrapers. How are the sounds different? Try sticking the sandpaper to hollow boxes instead of solid blocks of wood. You should be able to make louder sounds.

Make a Nail Xylophone

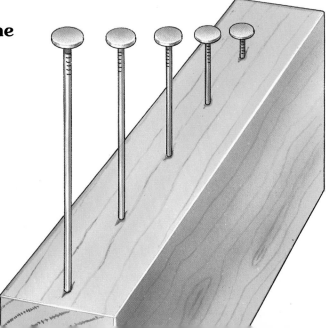

Ask an adult to help you bang some nails into a piece of wood so they stick out at different heights. Tap each nail with a metal spoon. Which nail makes the highest note? Which nail makes the lowest note?

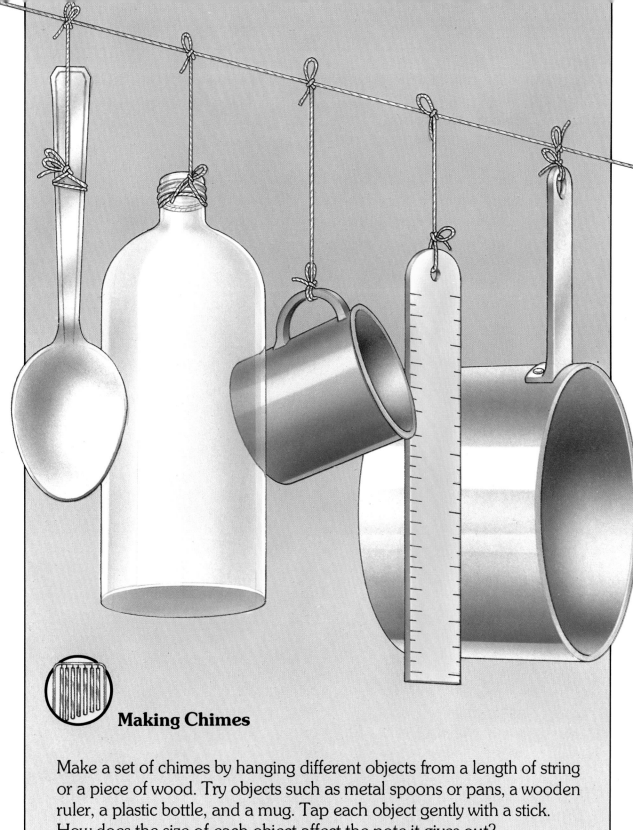

Making Chimes

Make a set of chimes by hanging different objects from a length of string or a piece of wood. Try objects such as metal spoons or pans, a wooden ruler, a plastic bottle, and a mug. Tap each object gently with a stick. How does the size of each object affect the note it gives out?

Shake, Rattle, and Roll

A shaker can be made from empty plastic bottles, margarine cartons, or small boxes. Collect containers that are different shapes and sizes and make sure they are clean and dry inside. Fill each container with small objects that will rattle around inside.

Fix the lid on the container with sticky tape and paint your shaker or cover it with wrapping paper. Which fillings make the loudest sound?

Here are some ideas for the fillings:

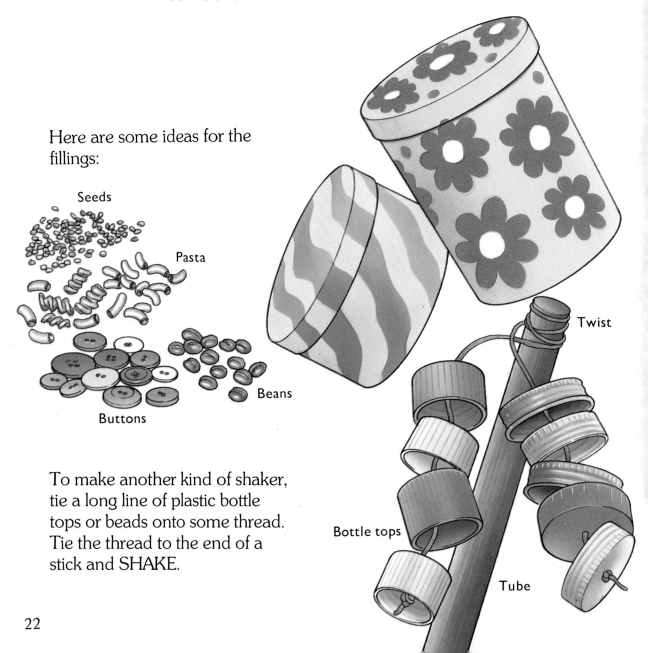

Seeds

Pasta

Beans

Buttons

To make another kind of shaker, tie a long line of plastic bottle tops or beads onto some thread. Tie the thread to the end of a stick and SHAKE.

Twist

Bottle tops

Tube

Making Maracas

1. Make small cuts around one end of the tube so it opens out flat. Glue this end to the bottom of one of the cups.
2. Pour the beans into the other cup.
3. Fix the two cups firmly together with plenty of sticky tape so the beans can't escape.
4. Paint or color the cardboard tube.
5. Hold the cardboard tube and shake to make a sound.
6. Make another one and shake your maracas in time with your favorite music.

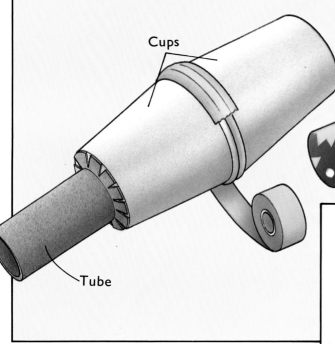

Cups

Tube

You will need:

two paper cups, a cardboard tube, dried beans, scissors, sticky tape, glue, paints or crayons.

Guess what's inside

Find a bottle you can't see through and choose one sort of filling to put inside. Can your friends guess what is inside the shaker?

MUSIC FROM PIPES

If you blow across the top of an empty bottle, you can make a musical note. This happens because you are making the air inside the bottle shake or vibrate. Musical instruments such as recorders, organs, or trumpets work in a similar way. The player blows into the end of a pipe and this makes the air vibrate and give out musical sounds.

Make a Bottle Organ

1. Collect several clean, glass bottles that are all the same size and shape.
2. Put the bottles in a line.
3. Fill one bottle with water almost to the top. Leave some air above the water.
4. Put a little less water in the next bottle and so on down the line. The last bottle should have just a small amount of water in the bottom.
5. Blow across the top of each bottle. Which bottle makes the highest note? Which bottle makes the lowest note?
6. With a metal spoon, tap each bottle gently. What happens to the notes?
7. Can you play a tune on your bottles? It is a good idea to put a number on each bottle. Then you can write down your music.

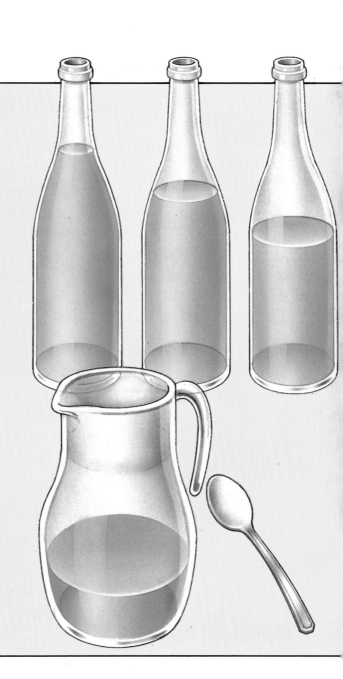

Singing Bottles

Find two clean, empty glass bottles that are exactly the same size and shape. Ask a friend to hold one of the bottles to their ear. Then stand about a yard away and blow across the top of the other bottle. What can your friend hear?

The vibrations of the air in your bottle trigger the same vibrations in your friend's bottle. So they should hear a faint note in their bottle. This is called resonance.

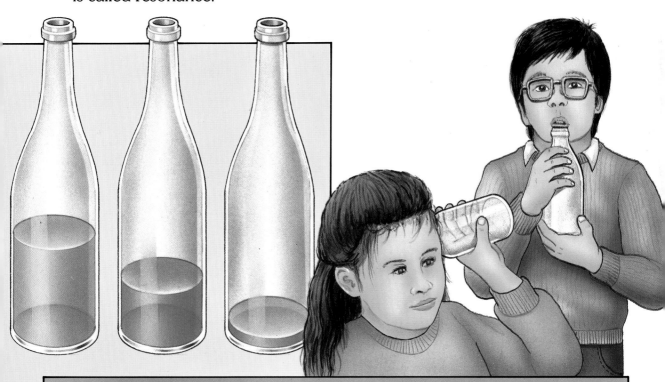

What Happens

When you blow across a bottle with a small amount of air inside, the air vibrates quickly and makes a high note. With more air in the bottle, the air vibrates more slowly and the note is lower.

When you tap the bottles, you make the water vibrate instead of the air. So the notes are the opposite way round. The bottles with a small amount of water give out high notes and the bottles with a lot of water give out low notes.

 **Make Pan Pipes**

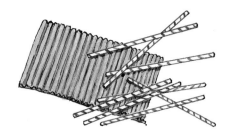

Pan pipes are a set of pipes that are played by blowing across the top. They are named for the Greek god Pan, who was half man and half goat. The music from his pipes was supposed to have power over all animals. The organ was probably developed from Pan pipes.

You will need:
a thin strip of corrugated cardboard, eight straws, scissors.

1. Push a straw through every other opening in the cardboard.
2. Cut each straw a different length with the longest straw at one end and the shortest straw at the other end. Make sure you have an even, sloping line, which matches the picture.
3. To play your Pan pipes, blow across the tops of the straws.
Which straw makes the highest note? Which straw makes the lowest note?

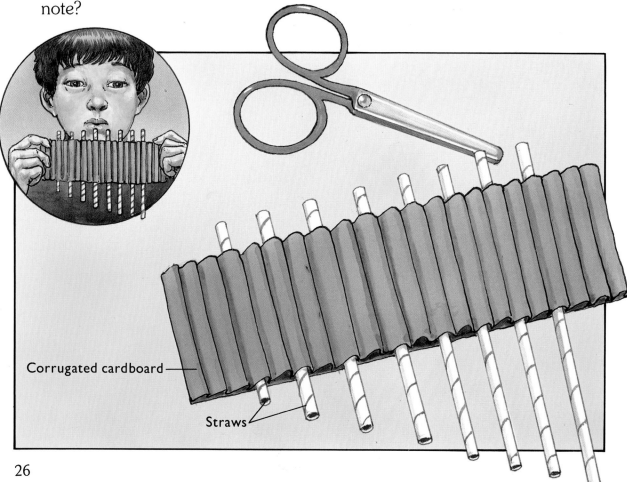

Corrugated cardboard

Straws

▲ If one pipe makes one note, how do instruments such as recorders make lots of different notes? A recorder has small holes at intervals along the pipe. When the player covers all the holes with their fingers, they are using one long pipe. When they take one or more fingers off the holes, they make the pipe shorter. This means they can play different notes.

Sound from Grass

Blade of grass

Hold a thick blade of grass tightly between your thumbs and blow hard. Can you make a screeching noise? The grass vibrates to produce the sound. This is what happens when a person blows on a reed in a musical instrument. Such instruments were originally all made of wood, and they are all played by the breath of the person, so they are called woodwind instruments.

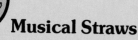

Musical Straws

1. Flatten the end of a straw and snip the end to make two points or "reeds." Now blow hard between the two reeds to set the air in the straw vibrating.
2. Keep blowing through the reeds while you snip off bits from the other end of the straw. What happens to the note?
3. To make a straw play two notes, cut a hole in one side of the middle of the straw. Bend the straw down to play a different note.

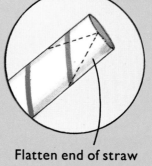

Cut off end like this

Flatten end of straw

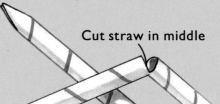

Cut straw in middle

Make a Trombone

Purse your lips and make a noise down a piece of plastic piping. Keep making the noise as you lift the pipe up and down in a bucket of water. How does the sound change?

A real trombone player pushes a slide on the side of the instrument up and down to change the length of the tube.

▼ Instruments made from brass, such as this trumpet, do not have reeds inside them. Instead, the player uses his own lips as reeds. When his lips are pressed tightly together, the air vibrates rapidly and produces a high note. He makes lower notes with his lips pressed loosely together.

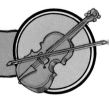

MUSIC FROM STRINGS

Stretch a rubber band around a book and put two pencils under the band. Pluck the band to make it vibrate and produce a sound. First try with the pencils a long way apart. Then move the pencils closer together. With a shorter length of band to vibrate, you will produce a higher note.

Musical instruments that produce sound by vibrating strings are called stringed instruments. Some, such as the guitar, are played with the fingers. Others, such as the violin, are played with a bow.

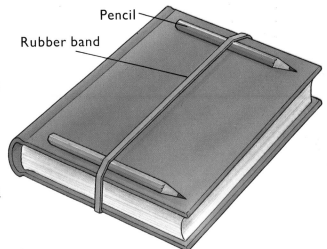

Pencil

Rubber band

Pinging Strings

1. Ask an adult to help you knock the nails into the wood to match the picture.
2. Pull one elastic band around each pair of nails.
3. Pluck the elastic bands with your fingers. Which bands make high sounds? Which bands make low sounds?

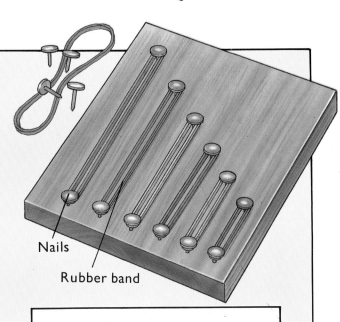

Nails

Rubber band

You will need:

a thick piece of wood, a hammer, some short nails, six rubber bands all the same size and thickness.

Make a Guitar

Collect together a large plastic box and eight rubber bands. Try to find long and short bands as well as thick and thin ones. Stretch the bands around the box and pluck them to make musical notes. Do the thin bands make higher or lower notes than the thick bands? If you use a bigger box or a smaller box, how does this change the notes?

What Happens

The vibrations of the bands make the air inside the box vibrate. And this, in turn, makes a lot of air around the box vibrate too. So you hear louder notes than from a solid piece of wood. This is why instruments with strings have a hollow box underneath the strings.

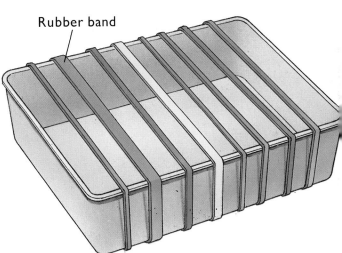

Rubber band

▼ Did you know that a piano makes music by vibrating strings? When the piano keys are pressed, little hammers hit wires inside the piano. This makes the wires and the whole piano case vibrate. The piano case makes the air around the piano vibrate too so it works like a giant sound box.

Stretching Strings

You will need:

a piece of wood, a nail, a hammer, string, a small plastic bucket, marbles or stones, two pencils.

1. Ask an adult to help you hammer the nail into the wood to match the picture.
2. Tie one end of the string to the nail.
3. Ask an adult to hold the piece of wood securely on a table. Put some marbles or stones into the bucket and tie this to the other end of the string.
4. Put the pencils underneath the string to lift it clear of the wood.
5. Pluck the string and listen to the note.
6. Now put some more marbles or stones into the bucket so the string is stretched tighter.
7. Pluck the string again. Is the note higher or lower this time?

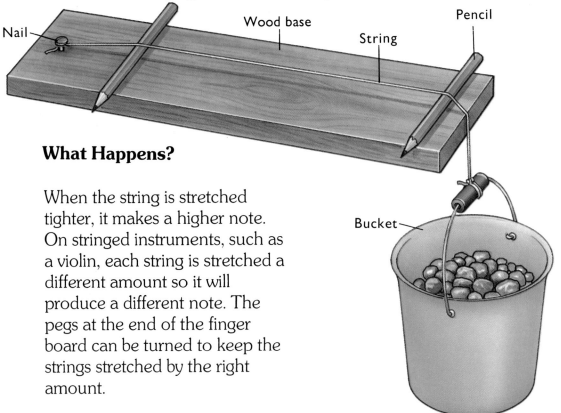

Nail
Wood base
String
Pencil
Bucket

What Happens?

When the string is stretched tighter, it makes a higher note. On stringed instruments, such as a violin, each string is stretched a different amount so it will produce a different note. The pegs at the end of the finger board can be turned to keep the strings stretched by the right amount.

◀ If you watch someone playing a violin, you will see that they often press the strings down with their fingers. This makes the vibrating part of the string shorter so it makes a higher note.

MAKING MUSIC

In an orchestra, the musicians make air vibrate to produce musical notes in three main ways—with strings, with pipes, or by hitting a surface. The size of the instruments affects the notes they make. Small instruments make high notes and large instruments make low notes.

In the picture, can you find examples of the different kinds of instruments? Look for stringed instruments (such as violin, cello, and piano), woodwind instruments (such as clarinet, flute, and bassoon), brass instruments (such as trumpet, trombone, and french horn) and percussion instruments (such as cymbals, drum, and triangle).

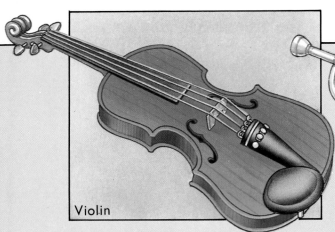
Violin

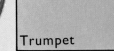
Trumpet

With Strings

In a stringed instrument, the note depends on the size and length of the string and how tightly it is stretched.

With Pipes

In woodwind and brass instruments, the note depends on the length of the pipe and the materials it is made from.

Drum

By Hitting Things

In percussion instruments, sounds are produced by striking with a special stick or hammer, or by hitting together the instruments themselves. Many of the instruments cannot produce definite notes but some can be tuned.

Sound Bounces Back

Try shouting into an empty bucket. Your voice bounces back from the sides of the bucket and the echoes sound very loud. In a concert hall or recording studio, the echoes can make it hard to hear the music properly. So the walls are usually lined with something that soaks up the sound. Cork, wood or heavy curtains are good materials for this job.

▼ In the Royal Albert Hall, London, disks in the ceiling help to reduce the echoes and make sound bounce back down to the audience.

Wrist watch

Props to hold umbrellas up

Umbrella Sounds

To investigate the way sound bounces off things, try this test.
Arrange two umbrellas to match the picture. Make sure that the handles
of the umbrellas are in a straight line. Fix a watch to the handle of one
umbrella and put your ear to exactly the same point on the other
umbrella. The sound bounces from one umbrella to the other in a
straight line and very little sound is lost along the way. So you should be
able to hear the watch ticking.

SOUND MESSAGES

Sounds gives us all sorts of information about our surroundings. The sounds people make tell us when they are happy, sad, angry, or frightened. Some sounds, such as music, are nice to listen to and may help us to relax. Other sounds, such as a police siren, carry an urgent warning message.

▼ The sound of a bell ringing is very useful for carrying messages. When a telephone rings, we know someone wants to speak to us. When a door bell rings, we know there is someone at the door. When an alarm clock rings, we know it is time to get up. Can you think of any other ways that we use bells to give us information?

Telephone bell

Doorbell

Alarm clock

▲ Fire engines need to get to a fire as soon as possible. They use a loud bell or a siren to warn other vehicles and people to keep out of their way.

▲ A rattlesnake makes a loud, buzzing sound by shaking the "rattle" at the end of its tail. This helps to scare off enemies, such as foxes. The rattle is made of old pieces of skin from the tip of the tail. The skin is hard, dry, and hollow. Each time the snake sheds its skin, another piece is added to the rattle.

▶ Frogs make loud calls by moving air to and fro across the vocal cords in the throat. When they push air against the floor of the mouth, it expands like a balloon. The air in the "balloon" vibrates and helps to make the sounds louder. Frogs call to attract a mate and recognize others of their own kind.

INDEX

Page numbers in *italics* refer to illustrations or where illustrations and text occur on the same page.

animal hearing *13*

banging *4*
bottle organ *24–25*
bottles, singing *25*

chimes *21*

drum *16–17, 34–35*
drumsticks *17*
  prayer drum *19*
  waisted drum *18*

earmuffs *10*
echo *36–37*

fire engine *38*
frog *39*

grass *28*
guitar *31*

maracas *23*
megaphone *15*

nail xylophone *20*
noise 10

organ, bottle *24–25*

paper snapper *11*
percussion *34–35*
piano *31*
pipes 24, *27*
  Pan pipes *26*

rattlesnake *39*

recorder *27*
rusting *5*

scraper *20*
shaker *22*
siren *38*
sound, direction of *13, 14*
  everyday *4–5*
  loud 10, 12
  messages *38–39*
  moving *6–7*
  quiet 10, 12
  underwater *7*
sound box *31*
splashing *4*
stethoscope *14–15*
straws, musical *28*
strings *30–31, 33, 34–35*

ticking *5*

trombone *29*
trumpet *15, 29, 34–35*

vibration *8*, 34

umbrella sounds *37*

violin *32*, 34
woodwind *34–35*

xylophone, nail *20*

Adviser: Robert Pressling
Designer: Ben White
Editors: Nicola Barber and Annabel Warburg
Picture Research: Elaine Willis

The publishers wish to thank the following artists for contributing to this book:
Peter Bull: page headings, pp. 11, 16/17, 19, 22/23, 30/31, 33; Peter Dennis (Linda Rogers Associates): pp. 6/7, 12–15, 26, 28/29, 36–39; Kuo Kang Chen: pp. 8/9, 20/21, 24/25, 34/35.

The publishers also wish to thank the following for providing photographs for this book:
31 A.G.E. FotoStock; 39 Pat Morris; 18 Jane Placca; 17 By courtesy, Premier Percussion; 36 Royal Albert Hall; 8 Hank Morgan/ Science Photo Library; 5, 29, 38, 39 ZEFA.

Published in 1990 by Warwick Press,
387 Park Avenue South, New York, N.Y. 10016.
First published in 1990 by Kingfisher Books Ltd.

Copyright © 1990 by Grisewood & Dempsey Ltd.

Printed in Spain

Library of Congress Cataloging-in-Publication Data
Taylor, Barbara, 1954–
  Sound and music/Barbara Taylor.
  p. cm.—(Fun with simple science)
  Summary: Describes how variations in the creation of sound can create musical tones for the human ear and why musical instruments produce sound.
  ISBN 0-531-19090-0
  1. Sound—Juvenile literature. 2. Sound-waves—Juvenile literature. 3. Music—Acoustics and physics—Juvenile literature. [1. Sound. 2. Music.] I. Title. II. Series.
QC225.5.T38 1990
152.1'5—dc20
89-78369
CIP
AC